Good-Natured Nina the Nervous Gnat

2

"The Sports Edition"

Good-Natured Nina the Nervous Gnat 2
"The Sports Edition"

Written by
Michael Finklea

Illustrated by
Vickie Sissel

Coastal Publishing
1025C W. 5th North Street
Summerville, SC. 29483
843-875-7775

Library of Congress Cataloging-in-Publication Data

Finklea, Michael, 1962-
    Good-natured Nina the nervous gnat 2 / written by Michael Finklea ; illustrated by Vickie Sissel. -- Sports ed.
   p. cm.
   SUMMARY: Coach Nina works with the school's sports teams, and some of the players are making her very nervous. She helps the players realize that working on positive character traits can help them to win more games.
   ISBN 1-931650-00-4

   1. Conduct of life--Juvenile fiction. 2. Animals--Juvenile fiction [1. Conduct of life--Fiction. 2. Animals--Fiction. 3. Stories in rhyme.] I. Sissel, Vickie, ill. II. Title.

PZ8.3.F623Goo 2001   [E]
                          QBI01 - 700578

Copyright 2001 by Michael Finklea
All rights reserved
Printed in the United States of America

I'm back! My name is Nina.
Why am I a nervous little gnat?
Read another little story and find out.

Exercise is very important.
Playing sports can be really fun.
It is okay to want to be number one.
But you cannot always be number one.
Just always try to be your best
at everything you do!

Read about Coach Nina as she works with the teams. See why some of the team players make Coach Nina a little nervous. Working on their character traits could help the players win their games. She does have two players that shine above the rest! Which player are you?

Leaping Lenny the lizard
Had some trouble sitting still.
Eager to begin the race,
He leaped against his will.

Coach Nina was not happy.
"*Leaping Lizards!*" we heard her squeal.
For the importance of being patient
Had been practiced in their drill!

Coach Nina's advice:

Patience!

TRACK

Side Line Sam the hermit crab
Had the speed but not the height.
Coach knew he could run the ball,
So she asked Sam to play one night.

Sam shuffled to the left
Then he shuffled to the right,
But he ran for the sand, not the grass,
And he shuffled out of sight!

Coach Nina's advice:

Participate!

FOOTBALL

Have you wondered, Little Napoleon,
Why no one wants to play with you?
Maybe it's because you are just half an inch tall
But act like you are six foot two!

Look, no one likes a bully.
When you play a game, here's a clue:
You can still be a team player,
And the best at what you do!

Coach Nina's advice:

Play Fair!

Wrestling

Hem and Haw the song birds
Would only cheer the blues.
With nothing ever good to sing,
They were bearers of bad news.

If you have nothing good to say,
Don't say anything at all.
We want to support our team,
So go fly around a mall!

Coach Nina's advice:

Don't Complain!

They can't win.
They never win.

My feet hurt!

GO TEAM

Meet the Cheerleaders

His team was down by many points,
When Bubba heard the news.
They didn't seem to have a chance,
Thinking positive he would choose.

When Bubba took the center ring,
Even coach woke from her snooze.
This tiny little ray of hope,
Big Bubba had the moves!

Coach Nina's advice:

Determination!

Boxing

We hope to count on Suzie
To swim the next relay.
But she may change her mind
And decide she doesn't want to play.

When Suzie joined our team,
She should not be so afraid,
To make sure she follows through
With the decisions she first made!

Coach Nina's advice:

Be Committed!

Swimming

When Sadie took position
With beauty, poise, and grace,
The crowd couldn't help but notice
She was the smallest in the race.

With pride she left in a blaze of dust.
We all thought, "For goodness sake!
She is going to win that first-prize ribbon
And a sugar apple trophy cake!"

Coach Nina's advice:

Believe In Yourself!

Horse Racing

"I won! I won! It's a lot of fun,"
Says the winner of the game.
Be very proud, but don't brag too loud.
A good sport would do the same.

It's not just about winning.
So if you're number one,
Applaud the other players
For the good job they have done!

Coach Nina's advice:

Don't Brag!

Cracker-Eating Contest

23

It's now up to each of you
To try and be your best.
Together we will be a team,
The secret of real success.

Always try and remember
What makes a superstar
Are the differences that set you apart.
So be proud of who you are!

Coach Nina the gnat

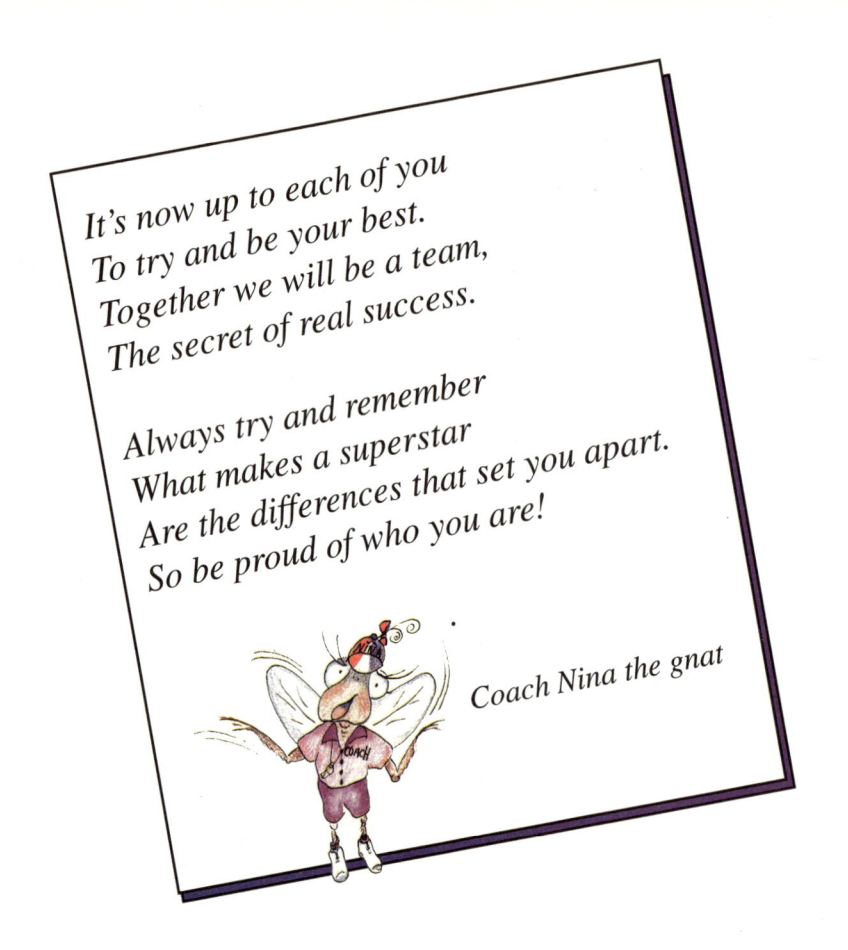

Those differences that set you apart make you an individual!
Be proud of those differences!
If you play on a team, be a team player!

24